USING
STUDENT
DATA

USING STUDENT DATA

{ Richard Selfridge }

CORWIN

1 Oliver's Yard
55 City Road
London EC1Y 1SP

CORWIN
A Sage company
2455 Teller Road
Thousand Oaks, California 91320
(800)233-9936
www.corwin.com

Unit No 323-333, Third Floor, F-Block
International Trade Tower, Nehru Place
New Delhi 110 019

8 Marina View Suite 43-053
Asia Square Tower 1
Singapore 018960

Editor: James Clark
Assistant editor: Esosa Otabor
Production editor: Sarah Sewell
Copyeditor: William Baginsky
Proofreader: Neil Dowden
Indexer: Melanie Gee
Marketing manager: Dilhara Attygalle
Cover design: Wendy Scott
Typeset by: C&M Digitals (P) Ltd, Chennai, India

Library of Congress Control Number: 2024909130

British Library Cataloguing in Publication data

A catalogue record for this book is available from the British Library

ISBN 978-1-5296-8580-0 (pbk)

TABLE OF CONTENTS

ABOUT THIS BOOK

Student data can be one of the most powerful tools a teacher can use to help their students to learn. In this book, Richard Selfridge offers practical advice for teachers on how to gather useful student data in the classroom and how to use these findings effectively to enhance your teaching.

- Authored by experts in the field

- Easy to dip in-and-out of

- Interactive activities encourage you to write into the book and make it your own

- Read in an afternoon or take as long as you like with it!

- Find out more at www.sagepub.co.uk/littleguides

Find out more at
www.sagepub.co.uk/littleguides

{ ABOUT THE SERIES }

A LITTLE GUIDE FOR TEACHERS series is little in size but big on all the support and inspiration you need to navigate your day-to-day life as a teacher.

 IDEAS FOR THE CLASSROOM

 HINTS & TIPS

 REFLECTION

 NOTE IT DOWN

www.sagepub.co.uk/littleguides

ABOUT THE AUTHOR

Richard Selfridge is a primary school teacher, data consultant and writer on education. His 2022 book for Sage, *Dataproof Your School,* written with James Pembroke, is a 'how to' guide for school leaders to use education data in schools. It builds on Richard's 2018 book for Sage, *Databusting for Schools*. Richard has worked with the Association of School and College Leaders, the National Association of Headteachers, AQA and the Independent Schools Examination Board, amongst many others, in his quest to develop data literacy in the education sector. Richard and James continue to work together, co-hosting the Databusters podcast and spreading the word at Data In Schools Conferences across England. In his spare time, Richard can be found hunting follies, usually by bike, or playing, listening to, watching, talking or thinking about music. He lives in Leeds with his wife Lindsay and daughters Martha and Connie.

INTRODUCTION

Student data can be one of the most powerful tools a teacher can use to help their students to learn. Building up a picture of each student's strengths and challenges during their time in school helps teachers to identify where their effort should be focused when working with large groups of students.

Having summaries of key data close at hand allows teachers to monitor, adapt and capture ongoing information on the students they are working with.

Key elements to using student data effectively and efficiently are knowing:

- What data you should have to hand

- How to summarise the data you have

- How to generate additional useful data

- How to identify what students know

- The questions you should ask of your data

- How to maximise the use of your data

This book will take you through each of these elements, sharing tried-and-tested classroom strategies and key research evidence.

CHAPTER 1
GETTING THE BASICS RIGHT – WHAT DATA SHOULD YOU HAVE AT YOUR FINGERTIPS AND HOW CAN YOU GATHER USEFUL DATA IN CLASS?

This chapter looks at the student data you need to make effective decisions in the classroom. Topics covered include:

- Making data accessible
- The student data you need to use
- Making the most of statutory data
- How to use standardised assessments effectively

As a teacher, you will be generating data on your students from the moment they enter your classroom until the moment they leave. You'll use this information in your work with students as you help them to learn what you want them to learn. Most of this information will be stored in your head and will never be formally collated.

You'll also have access to more information which has been collated and stored somewhere within the school system. Some of this information will be about personal details which might affect learning (contextual information), some will be attainment data (how a pupil has been assessed), some development data (how a pupil is progressing over time; their effort and attitude to learning) and some will relate to provision which has been put in place (specific adjustments to support a student's learning). You'll need to have this data at your fingertips so that it can help you in your decision making in class.

MAKING DATA ACCESSIBLE

You need to have access to useful summaries of student data which you can refer to quickly and easily as you teach. To do this, you need a number of seating plans (which contain specific information required for particular subjects or classes) and a one-page summary of the actions for specific students.

MAXIMISING THE POWER OF SEATING PLANS

For nearly every lesson, you need a data-rich seating plan. By selecting where students sit, and having key data at your fingertips for the lesson you are teaching, you maximise your ability to support those students who need more (or less) of your focus. Any additional adults in your lessons should also have access to this information so that they can maximise their support too. Some lessons – particularly for younger students – might be more unstructured (as might some lessons for older more mature students) but for most lessons, pupils will be sitting in a place you have chosen for them.

If you teach a subject to different groups of students, generate bespoke seating plans for each group. If you teach a class for the whole (or the majority) of the curriculum, you'll usually need seating plans for core subjects (maths, reading, writing) and a general 'home place' seating plan (you may need seating plans for particular subjects as you deem necessary).

Your seating plans enable you to both access key information you need to help you support the class and to gather further detail quickly and easily. Next to each student's name, you might include data selected from the list below:

- Age (as a date of birth)

- Age range

- Glasses wearer?

- Hearing or other impairments

- Pupil premium status

- SEND status

- EAL status

- Attendance

- Standardised score(s) for the subject

- Other assessment information

- Progress over time

- Attitude to learning

- Adjustments status (yes/no to indicate whether they need reasonable adjustments or not)

What you include on your seating plan will change over the time you work with the students. Once you have committed a particular set of key data – such as who speaks English as an additional language – to memory, you can move on to other data you need to know.

You can also gather detail using your seating plan, annotating your plan with specific information as required. This can then be transferred into whatever system you use to keep track of your class.

To really appreciate the power of a data-rich seating plan, put yourself in the shoes of someone teaching your class in your absence. If someone else takes your class, can they find the key information they need to know to enable them to work with the class effectively, quickly and easily on your plan?

HINTS & TIPS: THERE'S AN APP FOR THAT!

Whilst you could make your own seating plan on paper or a spreadsheet, you will find it much easier to use a tool which someone else has developed such as www.seatingplan.com, www.classcharts.com and www.clickschool.co.uk to create seating plans. One big advantage of using an online solution is that, once you have set up your class, you can easily manipulate your plans, making changes as and when you need to.

You will still want a paper copy so you can annotate your seating plan as you teach, so print one out for each class/lesson.

THE POWER OF A ONE-PAGE SUMMARY

A simple sheet of A4 paper split into four boxes will help you to both access key data and to record information about your class. Split the sheet into boxes with the following headings:

- SEND
- Knowledge, skills and understanding
- Actions arising from analysis of data
- Equipment/materials/resources

In the SEND box, record a summary of students with specific needs. It might look like this:

- AB – shortsighted; glasses; computer work (mornings), dark pen
- CD – hearing, left side
- EF – EAL, new to English, learning since (date)
- GH – Needs challenge in (subject(s))

For children with education health and care plans (EHCPs) or detailed special educational needs and disabilities (SEND) support, ensure that you have a summary of the actions you have agreed on the reverse of your one-page summary. For students with complex needs, have their summary documents to hand.

In the Knowledge, skills and understanding box, record specific areas which the class needs support to develop. These may include:

- Social/emotional skills, e.g. listening skills, speaking skills, developing empathy/respect for others
- Curriculum modifications, e.g. additional opportunities for maths fluency, phonics, reading, dictionary use

Actions arising from analysis of data may include additional support in class for specific individuals, e.g.:

- Regular check-ins
- Reasonable adjustments
- Resources/talk partners

Have a list of students whose reading is below a specific standardised score, plus those scores, e.g. IJ (78), KL (83)

Have a list of students whose maths is below a specific standardised score, plus those scores, e.g. MN (76), OP (84)

Use the Equipment/materials/resources box to list those items you intend to use to support learning and as a place to record those items you need to replenish or source for future lessons.

The reverse of the one-page summary is a good place to keep any additional data which might help you and your team to understand the class. This might include analysis of the age spread in the class or visualisations of key student data, for example.

 ## IDEAS FOR THE CLASSROOM

- *Use your seating plan in tandem with your one-page summary.* Each document is powerful but used together they ensure that you can access and capture student data efficiently and effectively.

- *Make your seating plans easy to read.* With an online seating plan app, you will likely be able to colour-code key information. You may also choose to annotate your printed plan with key groups or individuals.

- *Keep developing and keep track.* Seating plans and one-page summaries should be dynamic as you adapt to the needs of your students. Don't forget to keep track of the different iterations of your seating plans so that you can refer back to previous seating arrangements when necessary.

- *Keep a data-free seating plan to hand.* Students don't need to know how you have grouped them, so keep a data-free seating plan which students and others can refer to when necessary.

THE STUDENT DATA YOU NEED TO USE

You should have access to a great deal of the information below via your school's databases. Some of the data may not be held centrally; you will need to gather this yourself in class.

KEY CONTEXTUAL DATA: AGE, AGE RANK, WRITING HAND, VISION AIDS, ADJUSTMENTS, ETC.

Age in the form of a date of birth is key information; there are systematic differences between older-in-cohort and younger-in-cohort students. Whilst any individual may or may not conform to a population mean, knowing a student's age allows you as a teacher to check whether age may be a factor aiding or hindering a child's learning.

Are those first with hands up to answer questions simply the older, more experienced students? Are those reluctant to share ideas in class younger than their classmates? Are those chosen to represent the class students who have had more time to develop their confidence in speaking in public?

Of most interest should be the students who confound expectations, by knowing and understanding either more or less than might be expected. By having access to a student's age information quickly and simply, you can check your understanding of a child's learning and development as you teach.

Creating a simple age rank can make this process even easier. Knowing where a student sits in the distribution of the class is invaluable.

Given students generally sit at desks with others – often two sharing a desk – it is key that elbows don't clash when students are writing. Ninety per cent of students are right-handed, so knowing who writes with their left hand is vital. Left-handed students should of course sit to the left of a right-handed student.

Surveys suggest that two-thirds of adults in the UK wear glasses or contact lenses regularly, and a good number of students will need glasses to correct their eyesight. Surprising numbers of students don't realise their eyesight is not 20:20 and you should always be aware that students may not be able to see resources in the classroom.

Students who do have a diagnosed need for glasses should be recorded on your seating plan – it is surprising how many students 'lose' or 'forget' their glasses or claim not to need them.

Some students will have additional adjustments which need to be made to enable them to access the learning in your classroom. You will need to have access to this information in class.

You should have access to indications of disadvantage (free school meal/pupil premium status), special educational needs and disabilities (SEND status) and whether the student is recorded as speaking English as an additional language (EAL), as well as an indication of school attendance (with some commentary where necessary).

KEY ATTAINMENT DATA: STANDARDISED SCORES, ADDITIONAL ASSESSMENTS

As standardised scores indicate a student's general position within the distribution of the student population, they provide key information about past attainment. We will look later at ways of using standardised scores but for now, they are a key item of data which should be included in class seating plans and one-page summaries.

You might use the last standardised score a student recorded. A mean of the last three standardised scores might be more useful, or an overall mean of all the standardised scores the school has for the child. Having multiple scores (especially over multiple years) gives you greater insight into a child's position over time than a single score can.

Additional assessments may also be useful. This depends on your school's policies and practice. If you use general assessment groupings of some sort, you need ready access to this detail. For example, if you use a 'working towards age expectations, working at, working in greater depth' model, you should have easy access to this data in class.

KEY DEVELOPMENT DATA – PROGRESS OVER TIME, ATTITUDE TO LEARNING

Having an indication of a student's development to date is extremely useful, as is an indication as to whether a student is focused on learning what you want them to. Again, having the last snapshot might be useful; you may also use a mean of the last three observations or the overall score for the child.

PROVISION DATA – ADDITIONAL SUPPORT OR ADJUSTMENTS TO SUPPORT PUPILS

You should have easy access to details when pupils receive additional support and what this is. You should also have information on the adjustments particular students require to access learning in your class.

MAKING THE MOST OF STATUTORY DATA

Many schools require students to take statutory attainment assessments, and most collect key items of information about the students they teach. Those which are generated in schools and collated centrally are extremely useful provided they are used well.

Students in England should have the following statutory data stored in their school's pupil database:

ATTAINMENT DATA

As they progress through the school system, students will have:

- A phonics screening check score between 0 and 40; 32 is the expected standard achieved by 80% of students in Year 1 (the year they are six)

- A multiplication screening check score between 0 and 25, generated when students are in Year 4 (the year they are nine)

- KS2 scaled scores in maths and reading between 80 and 120 with an expected standard of 100, from SATs taken in Year 6 (the year they are 11). It is worth noting that these are not standardised scores and are generated using a different mechanism

- KS2 teacher assessment of writing, scored as working towards the expected standard; at the expected standard; above the expected standard (the year they are 11)

- GCSE grades, scored from 1 to 9, from assessments taken in Year 11 (the year they are 16)

CONTEXTUAL INFORMATION

Schools in England are required to collect information on a student's date of birth, attendance at school, pupil premium status (a proxy for socio-economic disadvantage relative to peers) currently and in the last six years, as well as special educational needs and disabilities (SEND) status.

ATTENDANCE DATA

Your one-page summary of a class should include key statutory data. The data you include will depend on your context; it may be information on attendance, on SEND, on attainment or other information deemed relevant for those teaching your class – see Chapter 5 for further advice and guidance on how to select the data you might include.

HOW TO USE STANDARDISED ASSESSMENTS EFFECTIVELY

Standardised assessments are formal assessments for which the administration, marking and scores have been standardised. Used effectively, they provide a time-efficient and useful mechanism for assessing students.

WHAT STANDARDISED ASSESSMENTS CAN HELP YOU WITH

The majority of paper-based, written standardised assessments are informed by classical test theory. According to this framework, results of assessments are effective at providing an indication of a student's rank within the population. As such, the result of a standardised assessment – a standardised score – provides a good sense as to whether a student is more or less typical of students of their age.

Standardised scores are reported using a scale which places the most typical result at a nominal score of 100. Results which are one standard deviation from 100 are allocated a score of 85 (one below) or 115 (one above). For more information about standard deviations, see Chapter 5 of *Databusting for Schools* (Selfridge, 2018).

Where a student is around or above 100, they are clearly keeping up with typical students of their age. Statutory assessments which use standardised assessments usually place expected standards somewhere between scores of 85 and 100. Students working above the standard for their age are usually those who score 110 and above.

Standardised scores are therefore useful to help you to understand where a student sits relative to their peers across the population. This helps you to avoid assessment based on comparisons between peers within a class or school; using standardised scores, you can quickly assess whether your class is more or less typical of a class in the wider population.

Standardised scores become particularly useful when they are aggregated over time. As standardised assessments are standardised for a particular time period (usually a school year or a term within the school year), results can be compared over time. A student who has recorded standardised scores of between 80 and 90 over multiple tests is systematically different to a student who has scored between 110 and 120.

WHAT STANDARDISED ASSESSMENTS CAN'T HELP WITH

Standardised assessments are not designed to assess what a pupil knows or has been taught in the previous few months. This may seem counterintuitive, as a great deal of assessment you might use is explicitly designed with this intention. Whilst standardised assessments are constructed from a series of questions (more properly, 'items'), and these questions are informed by the curriculum which a student is expected to have studied, those constructing a standardised assessment select questions based on their ability to discriminate between candidates, not their ability to assess knowledge of the curriculum.

A typical assessment will be constructed from a mixture of items which are based on both the curriculum taught in previous years (perhaps 80%

of the test) and the curriculum which students have been studying in the months leading up to the test. A relatively small number of items will be selected to discriminate between students expected to score less than 90. An equally small number will be selected to discriminate between those who score above 110. The majority of the items will be selected to discriminate between those students scoring 91 and 109.

On a typical 40-mark assessment, there may be five questions in the first and second category, with the remaining questions aiming to discriminate between those in the middle.

The questions are selected to *discriminate between candidates* and not to *assess what they know*. Given this is the principle which underpins standardised tests, it should be clear that placing too much weight on the knowledge which appears to be assessed by a standardised assessment is likely to be counterproductive if your goal is to develop students' understanding of a given subject.

Knowing this will help you to use standardised scores in a way which is warranted; use scores to check against your own assumptions as to a student's development. Scores which encourage you to question your assumptions are worth investigating. Those which agree with your teacher assessment are extremely useful as they indicate your effort should be focused elsewhere.

Some assessments which have their administration and scoring standardised are not constructed from items as described above. Examples include England's phonics screening check and multiplication screening check which are constructed using a slightly different methodology. For these kinds of assessments, it is still worth remembering that the items are designed to rank pupils and not to assess their knowledge of specific aspects of the curriculum.

 # REFLECTION

Think about a class or subject you teach. What information would be most useful to have on your seating plans and one-page summaries?

How could technology help you to generate and maintain your seating plans?

What have you learned about the limitations of standardised assessments? What have you learned about their benefits? How might you use the results of standardised assessments in future?

NOTE IT DOWN

DECIDE WHICH STUDENT DATA WILL BE ON YOUR SEATING
PLANS AND YOUR ONE-PAGE SUMMARIES.

	CAN ADD NOW	CAN GET	NEED TO GENERATE
AGE			
AGE RANK			
WRITING HAND			
VISION AIDS			
ADJUSTMENTS			
FSM/PP STATUS			
EAL			
SEND STATUS			
ATTENDANCE			
OTHER (RECORD WHAT BELOW)			

STANDARDISED SCORES

- LAST ASSESSMENT?

- ONE-YEAR MEAN?

- OVERALL MEAN?

- COLOUR CODED?

ADDITIONAL ASSESSMENTS

- (RECORD NAME BELOW)

- COLOUR CODED?

Progress over time

- Last recorded?
- One-year mean?
- Overall mean?
- Colour coded?

Attitude to learning

- Last recorded?
- One-year mean?
- Overall mean?
- Colour coded?

Additional support

- Time + dates
- Details (record below)

Adjustments (record below)

CHAPTER 2
GENERATING DATA IN CLASS – WHAT ELSE DO YOU NEED TO KNOW?

This chapter looks at the student data you can generate yourself by asking students to complete simple tasks, through your own observations in class and conversations with students and other staff in school. Topics covered include:

- What can students do?
- Who is putting in the effort and learning what you want them to?
- What is getting in the way of learning?

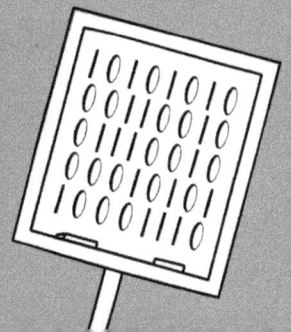

Students will have learned a huge amount which is not captured in the datasets you have access to. Much of this will relate to their ability to read, write and work with numbers. Quick and easy assessments of pupils' key knowledge, skills and understanding are vital so that you can put in place support where it is needed.

Knowing which students are not working hard in school is key to supporting those students who are not making the most of their time. For those who are finding learning difficult, you need to work out what you think is getting in the way and how you might minimise obvious barriers to learning.

WHAT CAN STUDENTS DO?

Your students need to be able to record their ideas at an age-appropriate level of written work. There are some core aspects of their written work which you will need to assess to support your work with a class. Students also need to be able to access written materials in order to understand tasks and to develop their understanding of a subject. You need to understand your students' ability to access the written word and to find out what they can do. Some key knowledge underpins both maths and those subjects which require use of mathematical understanding. You need to generate useful data to assess what students can do in each of these aspects of learning.

You will, of course, need to adapt the following ideas depending on the age and stage of the students you teach.

KNOWLEDGE FOR WRITING DOWN IDEAS

Surprising numbers of students either do not internalise or cannot recall some key aspects of writing which they have been taught. The root cause of writing containing non-standard formatting (such as not using paragraphs) and grammar is often students' lack of knowledge of the conventions of written language.

USE A SIMPLE ASSESSMENT TASK TO ASSESS KNOWLEDGE OF LOWER- AND UPPER-CASE LETTERS

Have students write out the alphabet in lower and upper case at the back of any book they write in. Use this to check for understanding of letter formation. Where you find ill-formed or missing letters, incorporate teaching of these into your work with the class.

Likewise, assess pupils' ability to use numerals and key mathematical symbols by having them write a dictated list into the back of any maths or science book. Teach what needs to be taught.

Students should write both the symbols and names of key punctuation marks at the back of their books.

Check understanding of paragraphing and formatting by using regular dictation exercises. This will also help students to internalise the content of the passages you choose for these exercises.

CHECK UNDERSTANDING OF ESSENTIAL GRAMMAR

This is particularly important where there are significant differences between children's speech and written standard English. Some languages do not use definite articles, for example, and some vernacular speech differs from standard English.

READING SPEED/COMPREHENSION SKILLS

Students need to be able to read reasonably quickly with sufficient comprehension in order to use written materials in their learning. You will need to make your own judgement of the level you require for both reading speed and comprehension. The following tasks will support you in your assessment.

- *Two-minute reading task – decoding*. Group students into pairs. Have student A read a passage you have selected out loud to their partner.

The partner's role is to check a student is reading each sentence accurately. Where a student reads a word incorrectly, they should repeat the entire sentence correctly before they move on. After two minutes, student A should count the number of lines they have read and multiply this by ten (more advanced students can find a rough mean number of words per line and multiply by this, practising their maths skills as they do). Record the number of words and the date at the back of an exercise book. Repeat the exercise for student B.

• *Two-minute reading task – maximum words per minute*. Again, group students into pairs. Have student A read a passage out loud to their partner as quickly as they can. Where the student reads a word incorrectly, student B ensures that student A repeats the entire sentence correctly before they move on. After two minutes, calculate words read as above. Record the number of words and the date at the back of an exercise book. Repeat the exercise for student B.

• *Reading comprehension*. Assessing reading comprehension is more complicated; if you have access to reading scores from earlier comprehension-focused assessments, use these to inform your decisions. If not, consider sourcing comprehension tasks which will allow you to group pupils in broad categories to allow you to focus your support for the class.

KNOWLEDGE FOR WORKING MATHEMATICALLY

As mathematics is a hierarchical subject, the further students progress through the curriculum, the more that has to be assumed about their key knowledge and understanding. It is necessary to check that key understanding to enable you to plan effectively to support future learning.

Students need to develop arithmetical fluency-near instant recall of key arithmetical knowledge. What your students should know will depend on the stage they are at. The following is a rough sequence of learning which students should internalise:

• Number bonds to 10; number bonds for all numbers to 10 then 20; partitioning numbers efficiently; adding and subtracting fractions and decimal fractions

- Multiplication and division facts for all one-digit x one-digit calculations; multiplication by 10, 100, 1000 and so on; division by 10, 100, 1000 and so on; common square numbers

- Knowledge of prime numbers, factorising and finding common multiples

Much of this knowledge can be assessed quickly during short activities in class, such as an opening task set as students prepare for a lesson. If your school uses an online mathematical fluency tool, such as TT Rockstars or XtraMath, use its assessment tools to help you identify students who may need additional resources, support or teaching.

Simple quizzes based on your curriculum can be used to identify students who may need additional resources, support or teaching. You can generate these quizzes yourself or use the increasingly sophisticated large language models which are available to create outline quizzes for you to edit.

- *Standard algorithms.* Whilst you should be encouraging students to calculate quick and efficient answers using a range of techniques, understanding and being able to use standard algorithms to check answers to standard calculations using all four operations is a key skill and should be assessed regularly.

  Make a checklist of how you expect students to use the standard algorithms for addition, subtraction, multiplication and division. Collect examples of student work which exemplifies your expectations and make these available to students – unlike the written work in humanities subjects, students may not regularly see clear, well-formatted written mathematics.

  Set regular tasks using numbers to suit the level at which you are teaching. Ensure you use zeros within multidigit numbers and decimal fractions as appropriate to check students' understanding and ability to work with higher order problems.

  In subjects which require calculations, have students record at least one example of each of column addition, subtraction, short and long multiplication and short and long division.

- *Written mathematics.* As noted above, many students will not regularly read mathematics written by anyone other than their teachers and themselves. As a result, students regularly develop idiosyncratic habits in their written work.

  Make a checklist of how you expect students to record their work. How should students space their writing? If their workbooks include squared paper, how should numerals and words be written? When and why should a student write on the next line? When and why should they miss a line, underline or score through work? Should students write in pen or pencil? If they use pencil, when should they use an eraser? How should students indicate a final answer?

  Collect examples of student work which exemplifies your expectations, annotate them to make clear what you expect and make these exemplars available to students.

  Use regular written tasks which require students to both calculate an answer and explain their thinking. Use these tasks to identify errors and misconceptions.

 ## IDEAS FOR THE CLASSROOM

- *Build a list of the information which you find useful.* Use the ideas above as a starting point to help you to decide what you can gather in class.

- *Keep refining your list.* Add and remove areas as you feel necessary; as you get to know a class, keep thinking about what information you might need to gather.

- *Revisit tasks at regular intervals.* If you checked something in September, make sure you revisit it later in the academic year.

USING OBSERVATIONS AND CONVERSATIONS

Whilst a great deal of the useful data you need will come from written assessments planned in advance or from a detailed understanding of the curriculum students are being taught, further information can be generated during your day-to-day time with students via your own observations and conversations with both students and other staff.

WHO IS PUTTING IN THE EFFORT AND LEARNING WHAT YOU WANT THEM TO?

Generating and collating useful teacher assessments of aspects of a student's approach to school can be quick, easy and incredibly useful. Being able to look back on a student's progression through your school can help to identify ways in which you might make adjustments to support their future learning in your class.

One key area which you should be monitoring is the effort a student is making during their time in class, and the effect of that effort.

- Quick and easy attitude to learning scores
- The power of quizzing
- Use tech to help you

QUICK AND EASY ATTITUDE TO LEARNING SCORES

Generating and collating attitude to learning scores is routine in secondary education, when students are typically taught by several teachers. Schools know that collating this information can help to identify any areas of the curriculum in which a student is showing a lack of effort.

Typical attitude to learning scores are generally very simple. Students are scored using a Likert scale, with five options. These can take many forms. For example, a student can be scored using descriptors such as:

- Ambitious

- Active

- Passive

- Reluctant

- Resistant

Each descriptor can be allocated a numerical value (5 to 1, say) to enable very simple analysis over time. You may want to develop a rubric for each descriptor to ensure some consistency, although this is not always necessary provided the scores are treated with the caution which this guide will advise when it comes to making inferences from data.

In a primary setting, where a teacher teaches multiple subjects, you may wish to generate scores in key subjects such as reading, maths, writing and science. In secondary, where you are generally teaching one or two subjects, you should generate scores for each subject.

How often you collate scores is up to you. Many schools generate this kind of data on a termly basis. You may do this initially; once your systems are in place, you might want to reduce this frequency. Generating scores should take less than five minutes; start by scoring all students as Active (4) and then change students based on your observations of their effort and attitude in class.

THE POWER OF QUIZZING

Much has been written about what has come to be known as *retrieval practice* (Perry et al., 2021). In summary, there is evidence that activities which require students to recall information from memory can have a positive effect on learning. In addition to this, students' efforts and results from retrieval practice activities can also build a picture as to whether students are trying to learn what we want them to.

Many teachers use this kind of approach in their classroom, incorporating questioning designed to enable students to practise recalling information or to use skills, techniques and procedures which have been previously taught.

Quizzing, in which all students are asked to answer a limited number of questions in a short period of time, can generate information about multiple students quicky and easily. Capturing that information can be tricky – there are usually 30 sets of answers and just one teacher observing, so you will have to focus your attention on a limited number of students. That said, you can use quizzing safe in the knowledge that it will be helping many students embed their knowledge and understanding as well as helping you to understand which of your students is making an effort.

Quizzing generates useful information on what a student can do during or following a lesson. In Chapter 3, we will look at some of the questions about whether quizzing assesses long-term retention of information. But for now, quizzing is certainly a useful indication as to whether a student has either struggled with a new concept or has been trying to learn in class or not.

Whilst collating information from quizzing requires some time and effort, it can be extremely useful when it comes to informing your attitude to learning scores. It also becomes much less onerous and more efficient the more you do it.

 # HINTS & TIPS: USE TECH TO HELP YOU

And whilst collating information generated via quizzing requires effort, many people have developed systems to allow a busy teacher to collate useful data quickly and easily. The simplest of these systems use a single device to capture answers to quizzes (plickers.com, for example, uses an ingenious method of collating answers to questions from an entire class). Other systems (such as carousel-learning.com) allow students to enter answers on a device either in or outside of the classroom (at home, for example).

(Continued)

Tech can also help busy teachers generate quiz questions; many systems include vast databases of previously created questions. Large language models using artificial intelligence are particularly useful when it comes to generating first drafts of questions based on the material you have taught, which you can then refine for the classes you teach.

WHAT IS GETTING IN THE WAY OF LEARNING?

In generating attitude to learning scores and seeing responses to quizzes, you will begin to build a picture of students who aren't always focused or who have been unfocused in the past. The next question should be: what's getting in the way?

- Ask them!
- Use your SENDCo

ASK THEM!

For students who are scoring less than 4 on your attitude to learning scale, take time to find out what they think is getting in the way. Depending on their age and disposition, their answers might provide a lot of useful insight which will help you to help them. Their answers may also help them to be more aware of what inhibits their learning. Here are some questions you might want to consider:

- Who are your friends in class?
- Do you work well with them?
- Who don't you work well with?
- Who do you work with best?
- Are there times when you find it easier to focus?
- Are there times when you find it harder to focus?

- What has helped you in the past?

- What would you like to help you in the future?

USE YOUR SENDCO

Special educational needs and disabilities coordinators (SENDCos) are an invaluable resource when it comes to students with identified – or emerging – additional needs. Don't forget that pupils are developing all the time and that needs often diminish or intensify. The typical picture in many schools is pupils entering with speech, language and communication needs, which then either become less of an issue over time or develop into cognitive, social and emotional and mental health needs as a student moves through school. At a population level, more boys than girls have education, health and care plans (EHCPs) at all ages; there is a steady increase in the number of children with EHCPs through to the end of primary education, at which point the number of EHCPs stabilises. By the time students move into secondary school, there are three boys for every girl amongst those with EHCPs. Of course, individuals in your class won't always follow these population level trends.

You should therefore be aware that those with identified special needs may be finding ways to manage the needs they have. Some may be on course to require an EHCP. Some students will be developing additional needs and may need support in your class now or in the future. Other students have more complex needs that require additional support.

Your SENDCo will be able to advise you where necessary. Make sure you keep them updated as to your observations in class, checking in every three to six weeks.

 REFLECTION

Think about a class you have taught recently. How much did you know about your students' knowledge of key skills in reading, writing and arithmetic? Did you know of any specific needs for

(Continued)

students? What did you begin to realise was important after you had worked with them for a term or so?

How could you ensure that you built in tasks to assess key knowledge and skills as early as possible in your time with the class?

Think again about the class or subject you teach. Make lists of the children you think are ambitious, active, passive, reluctant and resistant.

Make a list of any education technology resources you use. Search for new tools and see if you can add them to your list in the next week.

Think of students you rated as less than ambitious above. Think of questions to ask them. When you've asked the first of your students your questions, repeat the exercise with the others.

Make a list of things you want to discuss with your SENDCo and talk to them about what you are doing in class.

NOTE IT DOWN

Create an outline plan for the information you would have generated in class for a group of students you teach at the moment or have recently taught.

CHAPTER 3
SUBJECT-SPECIFIC KNOWLEDGE – WHAT DO STUDENTS KNOW IN DIFFERENT SUBJECTS?

This chapter looks at tracking subject-specific knowledge around which your curriculum is based. Topics covered include:

- Making decisions about subject knowledge
- How should you gather data?

MAKING DECISIONS ABOUT SUBJECT KNOWLEDGE

As you will have seen in Chapter 1, standardised assessment is not designed to assess a pupil's knowledge or understanding of the curriculum; it is best used to indicate where a student's current performance sits within a distribution of their peers' current performance. This is certainly useful, but it does not help you to understand what a pupil knows in a given subject, and therefore how you might adapt a student's learning to support their development in school.

Chapter 2 looked at core skills, attitudes to learning and generating information about potential barriers to a student's learning in school. Here we will look at the key information which your curriculum intends students to learn and how you might assess it.

The student knowledge you need to assess in a given subject (or topic within a subject) will depend on the age, stage and subject which you are teaching. The information which those teaching five-year-olds need to track is very different to those teaching 15-year-olds. Equally, the information you need to track is systematically different when teaching more hierarchical subjects (such as mathematics and sciences, which build systematically on prior knowledge) as compared to less hierarchical subjects (such as history, geography and the arts, in which topics are much more loosely related to each other).

You need to know what will help you to make decisions about supporting students' learning in the curriculum you are intending them to develop their knowledge, skills and understanding. As such, it is essential to be clear about the key aspects of the curriculum you are intending them to learn. Identifying this information is the first step towards gathering the subject-specific knowledge you decide to track.

To assess specific subject knowledge, you need to understand what students should have been taught and what they should have learned.

WHAT SHOULD STUDENTS HAVE BEEN TAUGHT?

Whilst a detailed discussion of curriculum is beyond the scope of this book, you should be aware that a great deal of time and effort has gone into developing the curriculum taught in our schools. In England, the majority of schools have been required to follow the National Curriculum since its introduction in the 1990s, and schools' regulator Ofsted has had a huge focus on curriculum over the past few years.

Any written curriculum generally includes descriptions of the subject knowledge which we intend for students to learn during particular phases of their education. The National Curriculum is separated into multi-year key stages, with little indication of the curriculum content for each year of schooling, and so it is often difficult to decide what should have been taught – and learned – at different points in a student's journey through school.

However, your school should have a clear summary of the key information which students should have been taught in a given subject in a given period in your institution.

Over the years, a great deal of research has gone into understanding how humans learn. Cognitive load theory – summarised in *A Little Guide for Teachers: Cognitive Load Theory* (Ashman, 2023) – has given us greater insights into the ways in which we can help students to learn given the way in which our brains process and retain information.

In summary, whilst students' long-term memories are effectively limitless, they are constrained by the work they have to do using their working memory. In addition, working memory can easily be overloaded, making changes to long-term memory much less likely. Careful planning is required to ensure that students have the best chance of transferring what we want them to learn from their working memory to their long-term memory.

Identifying what we want students to learn and ensuring that both we as teachers and, ultimately, they as students know what this is makes the chance of students retaining the information much more likely.

WHAT SHOULD STUDENTS HAVE LEARNED?

Your school should have a well-defined curriculum which includes the key subject knowledge which students are expected to be taught and therefore to have learned. If you are fortunate, you will have some sort of summary of the subject knowledge students are expected to learn in a given topic within each subject.

If you do not have this, you should create one-page summaries of the knowledge you expect your students to learn in a given unit or topic of work. Once you have an existing summary, make sure that – based on your ongoing assessments of the students – you adapt it to ensure that it is both accessible and challenging for your students.

A useful subject knowledge summary will include some or all of the following, depending on the subject taught:

- Key vocabulary
- Definitions
- Key concepts
- Timelines, where relevant
- Labelled diagrams or images

Don't forget that, as students mature, these summaries can be powerful learning tools in themselves. By making what you want students to remember more explicit, students are more likely to ensure they work hard to remember that information.

 # HINTS & TIPS

What issues arise when we try to track student knowledge?

> **Simply put, performance is short-term, whereas learning is long-term. What this means is that teachers won't know if their students have actually learned something until after a period of time in which the students didn't use or think about the information. (Soderstrom (n.d.))**

You should be aware that when we attempt to track subject knowledge – what a student *knows* rather than what the student *can do* – we run into the difficulty of assessing performance rather than assessing learning. The distinction is important for a number of key reasons. Firstly, a great deal of work in the classroom is based on performance (as discussed in Chapter 2) as teachers try to help students work with ideas so that they retain the underlying concepts and information. Secondly, students may be able to perform well in the short term but find it more difficult to retain information in the longer term.

It is also useful to be aware of the effects of bias, which affect us all, whether we are aware of it or not. We have to make assumptions about students based on our prior experience of both the student and other students we have taught who may appear to be similar to a current student, and these assumptions will, in some cases, be wrong.

For these reasons, it is important to understand the limitations of attempts to track knowledge; it is difficult to be sure whether a student has retained something in their long-term memory or has simply retained it in the short term, and we may be wrong in our assumptions about the student.

That said, collecting data regularly and always asking whether you are wrong about your understanding of a student's learning can help to minimise the number of times you are likely to have made a mistake in your assessment.

HOW SHOULD YOU GATHER DATA?

Whereas using simple quizzing as discussed in Chapter 2 is a quick and easy way of gathering data, over time you should develop more intentional methods of gathering data from your classes.

USING INTRO AND OUTRO TASKS

Make the best use of the time it takes students to settle into a lesson by setting learning tasks based on your subject knowledge summaries which students must complete as the lesson begins. A simple 'Do now' task might consist of five items which pupils complete either in an exercise book or, if you have the technology, online. You can gather feedback on individuals, groups or whole classes through these tasks. Equally, use an Exit ticket system, in which students answer questions or provide feedback on their learning at the end of a lesson.

USING PUPIL SELF-ASSESSMENT

Simple systems of student self-assessment during lessons can gather a substantial amount of information. Set simple feedback tasks within a lesson which require responses on sticky notes (written feedback and student's initials) or via computer screens.

Give students opportunities to indicate what they know or want to know using Know/Want to know charts – use a simple system (sticky notes work well here) to allow students to respond to whole-class questions posted on a wall in your classroom.

The main advantage of gathering feedback using these methods is that you can easily collate and store the feedback, rather than having to search through books to find student responses.

USING HOMEWORK

Whilst there are many arguments both for and against homework, for some students work done outside of the classroom can provide effective feedback on students' effort and learning. Consider how you will collate any feedback you gather this way so that you are able to set tasks which require minimal administration once submitted.

Consider whether written or online tasks will be more efficient for your purposes. For some subjects such as maths, science and reading, there are many efficient online tools which will help you build a picture of students' knowledge and understanding. For other subjects, there are many online platforms (such as Carousel Learning) which allow you to create online quizzes based on the material you have taught.

Expect a high response rate from most of the methods above but recognise that some students may not complete feedback for whatever reason; gather feedback from these students in person in the next session.

USING WRITTEN ASSESSMENTS TO IDENTIFY STUDENT KNOWLEDGE

Written assessments can be useful to allow students to show what they can do. They can help to limit bias, particularly when they have been standardised as discussed in Chapter 1. They may still capture performance rather than learning, however, particularly if they assess knowledge which has been taught recently as discussed above and in Chapter 2. Put simply, a student may be able to answer questions on material they have just been working on but may not be able to do so a few weeks or months after they last encountered it.

 IDEAS FOR THE CLASSROOM

- *Integrate data gathering into your planning.* Consider which key information you can collect during each lesson and make sure you include opportunities to gather feedback from students in class.

- *Use your support staff.* If you have additional adults in class with you, let them know what information you'd like them to gather during a lesson. If your support staff are able to manage independent whole class work, work with individuals or groups yourself.

(Continued)

- *Have students self-reflect in their books.* Have students record what they have learned or found out in a lesson or series of lessons by asking them to complete simple sentences such as, 'I have found out that…' or 'I have got better at…' Gather their responses as a class and keep a note of their feedback.

 # REFLECTION

Think about a unit or topic within a subject which you have taught recently. How clear were you about the subject knowledge you wanted the students to learn? How clear did you make this to students? Did the students know what subject knowledge they were expected to retain?

How could you ensure that you built in tasks to assess key knowledge and skills during your time with the class?

What have you learned about the difference between performance and learning? How could you use this information to help you in future?

NOTE IT DOWN

CREATE A SUMMARY OF THE KEY SUBJECT KNOWLEDGE YOU WANT STUDENTS TO LEARN DURING A UNIT OF WORK YOU ARE PLANNING TO TEACH.

CHAPTER 4
USING DATA TO ASK QUESTIONS – WHAT SHOULD YOU WANT TO KNOW?

This chapter looks at the questions you should ask in order to use student data effectively in your teaching. Topics covered include:

- What do you know about your students?
- What challenges do your students face?
- Who's more complicated?
- Who should you be focusing on?

WHAT DO YOU KNOW ABOUT YOUR STUDENTS?

There are things you should take time to understand before you begin to teach your students which you can gather from the data that should have been collated within your school's databases. Knowing pupils' dates of birth, dates of school entry, prior attainment and attendance and so on is key to beginning to understand your classes.

HOW OLD ARE YOUR STUDENTS?

The mean age of the cohort and students' ages within the cohort provide useful data points when it comes to understanding a class. The middle of the English school year is 3 March. It is a simple task to create a list of students' ages in days relative to this and to find the mean difference between student's age and 3 March. Classes which are clearly older on average than those which are younger are likely be systematically different to each other.

As a group, pupils who are notably younger than their peers within their school cohort will have lower attainment and less-developed social skills. This effect is large when students are young but the effect is still present in older teenagers. Many providers of standardised assessments use age standardised scores in an attempt to mitigate this population effect.

Of course, every child is an individual, and population statistics do not dictate outcomes for any student. It is, however, useful to know whether, for example, a young autumn-born student is performing at a higher-than-might-be-expected level in their class.

Key question: Which students are in a surprising place in class, given their age?

You will find it useful to create an age rank list, which you can refer to when considering how older and younger students are developing in your classes. You should certainly be aware which the oldest and youngest students are prior to meeting your class.

Once you begin to work closely with a class, students' age ranks can help you to form an understanding as to whether a student is thriving or struggling in a given subject. You can also use this knowledge to help you assess whether a student might be masking a difficulty or minimising their effort.

Key question: Which students might be masking an issue, given their age?

WHO MIGHT BE NEW?

Information on when students joined your school can be extremely useful. Knowing what percentage of the class did not start learning with their peers can provide useful insight should this number be higher than you might expect. Experienced teachers know that pupils who start at the beginning of the school year are different to those who start at the beginning of subsequent terms, and those students are different to those who start at unusual times within a given term.

Again, these general trends may not apply to your students. But if this isn't the case, observing that will provide you with a useful insight into your class.

Key question: Who is new? Has student mobility had an impact on your class?

Should your school include new arrivals from non-English speaking countries, check to see if this information is collated within your databases. If it is, add it to your data toolbox to help you to understand the history of the class. Where pupils do speak other languages, check to see whether they have learned to read and write the language they speak. And where students speak at least one other language, check to see if they speak additional languages too.

Key question: Who speaks additional languages? What can they do in those languages?

PRIOR ATTAINMENT

In Chapter 3, we looked at the attainment information which your school might gather. As you will see, a great deal of attainment data is teacher assessed, which we know means that it is likely to be biased in some way, simply because assessment, especially of younger students, is difficult and prone to measurement error.

With this caveat, the data which is on your school's systems is a useful starting point to help you to understand the learning needs of a class. You might ask whether the assessments suggest the class as a whole is performing above or below their peers. You might also consider the spreads of attainment to understand any systematic differences which their prior attainment suggests – you may have two or three distinct groups, for example, or a number of key outliers.

It can be useful to rank attainment in subjects, and across terms/years if you have this data, and to look at patterns within students' ranks.

Key question: What groups, if any, do you have based on prior attainment?

Where your school does allow you to consider data over a longer period, consider any interesting patterns you find in the data. Have there been any systematic jumps forward or drops back? How many students have moved multiple places in the last few years? Are those at the top and the bottom consistently top or bottom in different subjects? And how does age interact with attainment ranks?

Key question: What attainment patterns might be of interest?

PRIOR ATTENDANCE

We know that attendance and attainment are linked at a population level, with pupils who have lower attainment being likely to have lower attendance compared to their peers and vice versa. Of course, any correlation does not necessarily imply causation, but understanding patterns of low attendance (and any known causes) can be useful.

In England, attendance below 90% is classified as 'Persistent absence' by the Department for Edcuation. This level of absence is more than one day a fortnight, and it is clear that students are missing substantial amounts of the curriculum if they miss this amount of schooling.

Of course, students as a whole do not attend every session in school; nationally, the authorised absence rate is around 5%. This is understood to be related to student illness and it is reasonable to use 95% attendance as a benchmark for most pupils.

As a teacher, you should know who has missed more than 5% and 10% of lessons in the last few years. Knowing a child missed school in previous years can help you to ask questions about their knowledge and understanding, and what support they might need in class.

Key question: Whose attendance history should you know about? What effect might it have?

WHAT CHALLENGES DO YOUR STUDENTS FACE?

WHAT MIGHT BE GETTING IN THE WAY?

The Education Endowment Foundation (EEF) has provided a great deal of useful insight into what might loosely be called the 'What works?' question. This insight is useful for you as it helps to ask what might be getting in the way of student learning. The EEF's guide to the pupil premium (2023) identifies three areas schools should focus on to best support students in school. These are teaching, targeted academic support and wider strategies.

In essence, the EEF suggests that we should focus on a solid integrated curriculum taught by well-supported professionals, specific support for those not thriving and support for children outside the classroom.

This might be further summarised by focusing effort to ensure that students are in school, in class, focused and learning what we want them to.

Your questions about your class should therefore focus on what might be getting in the way.

Key questions:

Have your students been in school regularly? If not, why not? What might they have they missed when they were not in school?

Are students regularly in class? Whilst some students may need to be taught separately for a number of reasons, how soon can they be integrated back into class? What needs to happen to keep them in class?

For those in class, are they actually trying to learn? Is anything getting in the way? If so, what is being done to help students to focus on their learning?

Finally, are students learning what we want them to? When they are assessed are they thriving? Is anyone doing better or worse than might be expected? Do we know why?

 HINTS & TIPS

This is an area which you will get better at over time. Whilst you are developing your skills, use more experienced staff to help you gain insight into the areas which students might struggle with. Make time to discuss your thoughts with others each week.

If you like reading, seek out books which might help you. Daniel Willingham's *Why Don't Children Like School?* (2021), Nancy Gedge's *Inclusion for Primary School Teachers* (2016) and Daniel Sobel and Sara Alston's *The Inclusive Classroom* (2021) are great places to start.

Don't forget to talk to your students about their experience of learning. Asking age-appropriate questions about their barriers to learning can help you to gain insight into a student's perception of their needs.

WHO'S MORE COMPLICATED?

Once you have built up a picture of students in a class, considering the student data you have and the challenges your students face, you will be able to focus on the students whose needs make their education more complicated.

WHICH CHILDREN HAVE OR HAVE HAD IDENTIFIED SEND? WHAT IS THEIR HISTORY?

As discussed in Chapter 1, your SENDCo will have data on the students in your class who have identified special needs. Your school should also have a system which allows you to see the history of support for children with SEND.

Where children have EHCPs, you should ensure that you understand what support has been specified. You should know when their first EHCP was put in place and how support has developed since.

You should also know which students have had support in the past but are no longer classified as having SEND.

WHICH CHILDREN ARE UNTYPICAL?

Not in school. As discussed in Chapter 2, schools are required to collect information on students' attendance and you should have access to historical attendance data. You should know which children have had attendance classified as persistent absence as discussed above in their time in your school. You should know which school year and term a student was absent for more than 10% of sessions. You should also know what their attendance was for these terms.

You should know if any child has had medical issues which have interrupted or affected their schooling.

> *Not in class*. Where your school systems have recorded any issues which have meant that a child has spent atypical amounts of time out of class, you should know which pupils were affected and when. You should have a summary of what these issues were.

> *Not focused*. As discussed in Chapter 1, knowing whether a student has been focused on learning what their teachers have wanted them to is key information, particularly when a picture is built up over time. You should know which students have had lower than average attitude to learning scores in any school year and term, and which years and terms these were recorded.

More advanced. Some of the students in a given class may be more advanced than their peers. You should check whether these children are simply those who are autumn born who might be expected to work at the higher end of the spectrum. You might expect your more focused students to be learning more too.

Depending on the stage in their education, you might consider additional support for your more advanced students to ensure that they are being given the level of challenge they need. As students move through the school system, there are increasing opportunities to provide additional opportunities for more advanced students, so consider whether you are able to provide these for the students working in greater depth than their peers.

WHO SHOULD YOU BE FOCUSING ON?

Having gathered the information above, you should prioritise the students who will need more of your focus. Whilst you are responsible for all of your students, it will be clear that some students require more focus to ensure that their prior experience in school is taken into account.

For the majority of your students, you will find that you do not need more than typical focus; you need to consider their learning needs as you would for any student you teach. By placing them in the broad category of 'Needing no additional support', you will free up your time for those who need more of your attention.

For this group of students, you should prioritise those who need your attention most whilst ensuring that you support those who need a lighter touch to help them to thrive.

Don't forget that students' needs change over time and that some students will move from one group to the other, either needing more or less focus as they move through school.

In summary, you should ask questions so that you can decide which students you should focus on in this order:

Those who your data suggests need active support now.

Those who have needed active support in the past.

Those who might need support in future.

Those for whom you have no additional concerns.

 # IDEAS FOR THE CLASSROOM

- *Keep a class diary.* Use an online document to record significant day-to-day information about a class: who's absent, who's out of class, who is not focused and so on.

- *Use transitions to reveal more about your class.* When entering or leaving your classroom, ask students to line up in a particular order. This could be birth order, for example, or number of siblings, those who have not missed a day of school in a given period.

- *Select a student of the day.* Each day, select one student to focus on. Using the data you have, ask yourself questions to check whether your assumptions about the student are reasonable.

 # REFLECTION

Think about a student you have taught recently who needed additional support to help them to access the curriculum. What was their biggest challenge? Was it to be in school, to be in class, to be focused or to learn what you wanted them to learn? What additional information would you like to have about that student? Could you access that information or would you have to gather it yourself?

(Continued)

How could you summarise what you need to know about a given class so that you can access the information during lessons? How could you develop your systems to streamline this process?

Which of your students are growing more independent? Which students might need more support? How many students are generally independent? How many need additional support?

NOTE IT DOWN

WHAT INFORMATION DO YOU WANT TO HAVE ABOUT THE NEXT NEW CLASS OF STUDENTS YOU ARE GOING TO TEACH?

CHAPTER 5
USING YOUR DATA EFFECTIVELY – HOW DO YOU MAXIMISE YOUR USE OF DATA?

This chapter looks at how to use your data effectively to focus your effort where it is needed. Topics covered include:

- Who is in school, in class, focused and learning?
- Who isn't in school and what are you going to do about it?
- Increase effectiveness and minimise effort over time

WHO IS IN SCHOOL, IN CLASS, FOCUSED AND LEARNING?

You should be clear which of your students do not currently need any additional focus to help them access the curriculum in your lessons. These are students who always perform well in any assessment task, are always in school and in class, and who are focused on their own development.

Depending on your class, you may find that you need very little additional information for this group. Where you do feel that you need to gather and collate additional information, make sure that it is information which you can use to make changes for this group.

Remember that students develop increased agency over their own learning as they mature and the older the students you teach, the more you should expect students to take responsibility for their own learning.

If you are able to provide additional challenge for your more advanced students, you should ensure that you include this in your class summary. You should make sure that you monitor this group for any changes over time. Where any issues arise, make sure that you record this in your class summary.

The students who are currently thriving provide you with the greatest opportunity to save time and effort when it comes to close assessment and monitoring which can be better spent elsewhere.

Analysing the data for this group and creating an action plan for them – even if your plan is to do nothing other than monitor the group informally – providing light touch support will free you up to focus on those who need it.

Don't forget that, at each stage of their education, most students are generally thriving within the academic curriculum. For most students, school works. Minimise the time and effort you take to monitor this group and focus on support for those students who need it.

WHO ISN'T IN SCHOOL AND WHAT ARE YOU GOING TO DO ABOUT IT?

For some students, the challenge is to be in school. You should work closely with others who support students with attendance issues. Depending on both your school and the students you are supporting, you may provide school-generated learning opportunities for students who have medical issues affecting their attendance.

If you are able to, ensure that key learning which is missed due to absence is recorded in your school systems, and that, when an absent student returns to school, they are given opportunities to engage with the learning they have missed. Timetabling short make-up sessions during breaks in the day can be an effective way for students to access key learning for which they were not in class.

Where students are missing lessons due to being out of class, consider how the lesson content which has been missed can be addressed. Keep track of key learning which has been missed. Can students work on condensed lessons during breaks in the school day? Can support staff work with students who have been out of class? Can key content be re-taught with the entire class at a later date once any issues have been resolved?

Where students are unfocused and not working hard to retain the information we want them to retain, consider what works to support these students. Would setting up regular communications between school and student's family help with their lack of focus? Does a student need to be placed at the front or the side of the class – or near an additional adult – for a period of time? Do they need a supportive peer for a time to help them to focus? Are there any underlying health, social or wellbeing issues which need to be addressed?

For all of these students, be careful not to reduce the student's agency to the point where they come to rely on others more than they should given their age and stage of development. The goal is to move the student to the point of maximum independence whilst providing the support needed to move the student as close as possible to the group which is thriving in school.

KEEPING TRACK OF THOSE WHO NEED SUPPORT

Your data will have enabled you to identify students who currently need additional focus and support. Once you have decided which students are in this group, you should create clear summaries of what you are doing to support their learning in the next few weeks and months.

For the majority of this group, these summaries do not need to be particularly lengthy. Do these students need more adult focus? Do they need access to additional resources? Do they need additional time for tasks?

A one-page A4 summary of your class which includes brief notes based on your earlier analysis of their needs will ensure that you and those supporting your class keep your plans for these students front of mind. The summaries should be working documents onto which you make notes of support you and your team have provided. Keeping these summaries will provide you with a record of the support students have had and help you when you come to create the next one-page summary for the class.

Change your summary as often as you need to ensure that you continue to adapt to the needs of your students. In particular, note where students are moving back into the group of students who are fine or where any students in the fine group are moving towards the group requiring support.

For students who have EHCPs, ensure that a summary of the support which has been planned is included in your day-to-day files. If you can include it in your one-page summary, then do so. If you need additional pages, ensure they are attached to the one-page class summary so that they are not overlooked.

 HINTS & TIPS

Decide how you will ensure you have access to your notes in the classroom. You can use a clipboard, a folder or a device such as a tablet for this. An A4 document folder which holds a writing pad, pens and pencils, and has space for loose papers,

is an excellent investment. Folders have the advantage of being relatively private as you can close them to prying eyes quite easily. If you do use a clipboard or tablet, ensure that your students know that they are yours and contain confidential information which is for your use and not theirs!

Having a single 'portable office' with all your notes and lists means you should always have access to the information which you need.

GETTING ADDITIONAL SUPPORT

Where students need additional support, make sure that you consider where that support may come from. Consider which other adults can support your students and discuss your situation with your SENDCo if you feel you need additional support.

Where other adults are able to support your students, make sure that you brief them clearly and provide a one-page summary of the support required.

Depending on the age and maturity of your students, you may be able to include the student themselves or other students within your additional support network. As always, the aim is to move from dependence to independence, so consider what you can do to support students as they become more responsible for their own development.

INCREASE EFFECTIVENESS AND REDUCE EFFORT OVER TIME

Always consider where your effort is best placed. Keep track of the more effective support you have provided. Use your judgement to decide which three or four of the reasonable adjustments you have made are working best.

Once you have decided this, consider how you might embed these adjustments into your class routines. How can you make these the responsibility of the students themselves? If particular resources are needed by some students, who can ensure that they are available and are being used? If students need regular check-ins, can you find a way to incorporate these into the students' own routines? Can you provide checklists for students which will help them to start tasks, to complete tasks or to solve regular issues they face?

Aim to implement changes which develop pupil independence as they become embedded. Your aim should be to ensure that additional support is in place and that you are enabling that support.

THE MORE YOU DO NOW, THE LESS YOU NEED TO DO IN FUTURE

Where current support includes any reasonable adjustments to be made in class, you should be clear what these are and who is responsible for ensuring that they are being delivered. In general, the model for ensuring reasonable adjustments are made is likely to be one which leads to greater independence for the student, so that, ultimately, students themselves take responsibility for their own learning needs.

Where students have provision in place outside of the classroom, you should know who is delivering this provision, as well as where and when this takes place. Keep track of any provision which is missed and the reason why it may have been missed so that you have a better understanding of the effectiveness of out-of-class provision.

CONCLUDING THOUGHTS

- Don't get overwhelmed
- Know what your data has revealed
- Take control of your pupil data

Schools are awash with data. There is a huge amount of information which is generated about students on a weekly basis and trying to track it all is almost impossible.

The demands of classroom teaching mean that it is all too easy to get overwhelmed by information, so make sure that you do not lose sight of the bigger picture. Keep focusing on the key questions – who is not in school, not in class and not focused. Of those who are, which students are finding learning difficult? What does your key data suggest you might be able to do for these students?

Make sure you know what your data might be telling you. More importantly, perhaps, be aware what your data can't tell you and where it might mislead you.

Always be aware that data helps you to ask questions rather than giving you simple answers. Start with these questions:

- What are the headlines for this group of students?

- What impact may a student's experience to date have had on their learning?

- Are assessment results what might be expected?

- Are there any surprises in the data?

Finally, take control of your data. Be sure that you know what you need to gather together and why this information might be helpful. Ensure that collating the data you need becomes more efficient over time. Develop your ability to analyse data so this becomes more efficient too. Focus on creating actionable summaries of the learning needs of the classes you teach so that you are making a difference where it is most needed.

 ## IDEAS FOR THE CLASSROOM

- **_Use checklists to help you._ Create a document with a list of all of the things you need to do each lesson/day – annotate your one-page summary, check your seating plans, select a child to focus on for the lesson/day, make up for absences and so on.**

(Continued)

- *Focus on developing independence.* Use a targeted support to independence model (adult verbal support → adult modelled support → adult prompted support → prompt → student independence).

 REFLECTION

Think about a class you have taught recently. Which students missed at least 10% of their timetabled lessons? What key learning will they have missed? What could you have done to support them with that missed learning?

Think about a student who has not been particularly focused in class. How could you support that student to be more engaged with their learning?

Who can you turn to for additional support in your school? How could they best support your class? What could you do to help others in your school to understand the challenge your classes face?

NOTE IT DOWN

HOW CAN YOU HELP STUDENTS IN YOUR CLASS BECOME MORE INDEPENDENT?

REFERENCES

Ashman, G., (2023) *A Little Guide for Teachers: Cognitive Load Theory*. London: Sage/Corwin.

Education Endowment Foundation [EEF] (2023) *The EEF Guide to the Pupil Premium*. Available at: https://educationendowmentfoundation.org.uk/ education-evidence/using-pupil-premium [accessed 19 February 2024].

Gedge, N., (2016) *Inclusion for Primary School Teachers*. London: Bloomsbury Education.

Perry, T., Lea, R., Jørgensen, C.R., Cordingley, P., Shapiro, K. and Youdell, D. (2021). *Cognitive Science in the Classroom*. London: Education Endowment Foundation (EEF). Available at: https://educationendowmentfoundation.org. uk/evidence-summaries/evidencereviews/cognitive-science-approaches-in-the-classroom [accessed 19 February 2024].

Selfridge, R. and Pembroke, P., (2018) *Databusting for Schools: How to Use and Interpret Education Data*. London: Sage.

Sobel, D. and Alston, S. (2021) *The Inclusive Classroom: A New Approach to Differentiation*. London: Bloomsbury Education.

Soderstrom, N. (n.d.) Learning vs. Performance, Player Development Project. Available at: https://playerdevelopmentproject.com/learning-vs-performance [accessed 19 February 2024].

Willingham, D.T. (2021) *Why Don't Children Like School? A Cognitive Scientist Answers Questions about How the Mind Works and What It Means for the Classroom*, 2nd edn. Hoboken, NJ: Jossey-Bass.

INDEX